PLASTERWORKS

PLASTERWORKS

A BEGINNER'S GUIDE TO MOULDING
AND DECORATING PLASTER
PROJECTS FROM STARS AND CHERUBS
TO SHELLS AND SUNFLOWERS

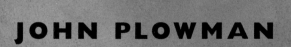

JOHN PLOWMAN

APPLE

A Quarto Book

Published by the Apple Press
6 Blundell Street
London N7 9BH

ISBN 1–85076–688–6

This book was designed and produced by
Quarto Publishing plc
6 Blundell Street
London N7 9BH

Editors Maria Morgan, Michelle Pickering
Copy editor Barbara Cheney
Art editor Clare Baggaley
Designers XAB Design
Blank plaster casts Mark La Trobe
Decorative backgrounds Mary Fellows
Plaster frames and panels Mark Jameson
Photographers Paul Forrester, Laura Wickenden
Prop researchers Jo Carlill, Natalie Rule, Anna Skuse
Picture manager Giulia Hetherington
Art director Moira Clinch
Editorial director Mark Dartford

Typeset by Type Technique,
121A Cleveland Street, London W1
Manufactured by Eray Scan Pte Ltd, Singapore
Printed by Leefung-Asco Printers Ltd, China

CONTENTS

INTERIOR DESIGNS

OCEAN WORLD

FACES AND FIGURES

INTRODUCTION

Welcome to the world of *Plasterworks*, where you will see how easy it is to make a whole range of decoratively finished plaster objects. Conceived with the newcomer in mind, this book shows you how to achieve truly spectacular results, from the functional Chameleon Clock to the ornamental Buddha Panel.

Plaster was used by many ancient cultures, for building, architectural decoration and sculpture, just as it is today. The modern type of plaster is made from the mineral gypsum which is ground into a powder. When reconstituted with water, it can be poured into a mould where it will harden to produce a solid cast.

Plaster, latex and paints are available from art and craft shops. You will be able to find most of the other items used here around the house; if not, your local

D.I.Y. shop will be able to help out. Blank plaster casts and ready-made moulds are also used in this book. These are widely available from craft shops and markets. Indeed, many museums produce

miniature casts of their masterpieces for you to transform for your own home and to give as gifts. If you are unable to obtain anything, a list of stockists is given on page 128.

The basic techniques of modelling, making a mould and taking a cast are explained clearly and concisely and require no previous experience. Everything can be done on a table top. Plaster casts can be decorated to suit all tastes and to match the ambience of any room. Here we will show you a whole range of possibilities which can be mastered by everybody, whatever their level of artistic experience.

You can be sure that whichever of these Plasterworks you choose to make it will add that extra bit of sparkle to any interior decor and, once you have learnt the basic but important techniques of casting and decorating, you will be able to experiment and explore ideas of your own. Happy Plasterworking!

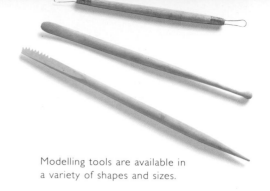

Modelling tools are available in a variety of shapes and sizes.

Clay and Plasticine are used to model original forms to be cast into plaster.

BASIC TECHNIQUES

MATERIALS AND EQUIPMENT

It is useful to have a variety of brushes. Use a spatula to mix plaster.

Most people know of two types of plaster: builders' plaster and plaster of Paris. Builders' plaster is very coarse and should never be considered for craftwork. Plaster of Paris is used here. The finest grade of plaster is "superfine". It is very hard setting and therefore ideal for casting. A softer grade, "fine" plaster is adequate for making support jackets for latex moulds and ideal for repair work. Both are sold under various trade names. Another hard setting type of plaster is decorating filler. This is a derivative of plaster of Paris and is used in some of the projects for freehand plasterworking.

Sealers and varnishes
Plaster is a porous material and will absorb paint quickly. If you are using spray paints or acrylics, it is not usually necessary to seal the plaster but for finishes such as marbling, where the paint must be kept wet, sealing is essential. A final coat of varnish will protect the decorative finish. Beware that plaster's porousness makes it vulnerable to the weather and so it is best to keep your plasterworks indoors.

White, "superfine" plaster is used for casting and a less fine quality plaster can be used to make support jackets for latex moulds.

A flexible mixing bowl makes it easy to pour plaster into moulds. It is cleaned by simply leaving the remaining plaster to dry and then bending the sides so that the dried plaster cracks and falls away.

Sealers and varnishes will protect plasterworks.

Decorative finishes

Most paints and staining mediums can be used to decorate plaster. Acrylic paints are ideal. They are quick drying and can be used in many ways: direct from the container; diluted with water to form washes; and mixed with specially manufactured mediums and with materials such as sand to create textures.

Brushes can be used in ways other than simply coating the surface evenly with paint. The dry brush technique allows you to apply highlights. First you load your brush with paint and then brush off the excess on a cloth or piece of paper; draw the brush over the surface and only the high points will pick up the paint. Stippling is another technique. Hold your brush vertically and dab downwards.

However, paintbrushes are not the only implements you can use to apply paint. You can spatter your cast by loading a toothbrush with watery paint, drawing back the bristles and releasing.

Sponges can be used in two ways which will recreate the pattern of their surface texture on the cast: dab a colour on top of another or dab a dry sponge on top of wet paint to remove some of the colour. Cloths can be used to wipe paint over the surface highlights of a cast.

Working area

Cover your working area with newspaper – it is the easiest way to clear away spilled plaster and is essential for decorative techniques such as spattering. Always have cleaning materials to hand; use white spirit to clean oil-based products and soap and water for water-based ones.

Acrylics and spray paints are ideal for plaster. Use toothbrushes, sponges and cloths as well as paintbrushes to apply paint.

Metallic paints come in many forms and produce beautiful finishes.

Latex is a flexible mould-making material which picks up fine surface detail.

Scrim adds strength to large casts.

Powder paint is used to make coloured plaster.

MIXING PLASTER

A good mix of plaster is essential for any plaster project. A bad mix results in a weak plaster – that is, if it sets at all! To produce a good mix the correct amount of plaster needs to be added to the water. Weighing and measuring play no part as the process itself indicates when to stop adding plaster. This method is foolproof, easy to learn and always produces a good mix.

Feel the heat

When plaster and water are mixed together an exothermic reaction takes place, i.e. heat is given off. You can feel this after the plaster goes off (sets): place your hand on it and feel its warmth. At this stage the plaster is vulnerable and should not be disturbed. It will start to cool after a few minutes and although it will still be wet the plaster can be handled again. The time it takes to dry out completely depends on the size of the cast and the surrounding temperature.

Knock – don't wash

Working with plaster is a messy activity. Always make sure that both you and your work area are adequately protected before you start. Always clean your mixing bowl and tools after the plaster has gone off. Simply press the sides of the mixing bowl inwards and the set plaster will crack and fall away from the side of the bowl. Similarly, wait until the plaster has set on your tools and then scrape it off.

Disposal

You should never pour wet plaster down the sink or drain or wash wet plaster off under a running tap. When the plaster has gone down the drain it will almost certainly go off, resulting in blocked pipework. If you wish to wash off wet plaster always have a bucket of water at hand to do this. At the end of the work session allow the solid stuff to settle to the bottom, pour the water down a land drain and dispose of the solid waste in the household refuse.

Gently sprinkle the plaster as close to the surface of the water as possible. Disperse it slowly and evenly over the surface.

The plaster sinks to the bottom but as you add more it will gradually start to rise above the surface of the water to form peaks. This is the characteristic to look for.

When peaks start to form allow them to settle for a few moments to see if they sink back into the water. If the peaks remain mix the plaster into the water, getting rid of any lumps.

A good example of a bad mix: not enough plaster has been added to the water. The plaster is transparent and immediately runs off the spoon.

Sprinkle some powder paint onto the surface of the water and mix well. Add enough colour to obtain the desired tone.

Your mix should be smooth and creamy. To test for a good mix withdraw a spoon slowly. The plaster should not run off the spoon and it should be opaque.

Colouring plaster

When making a coloured mix of plaster the colour should be mixed with the water before adding the plaster. Any water soluble paint can be used but it is easiest to use powder paint, as in this example. When you add the colour you should bear in mind that once the plaster is mixed the colour will be lighter than the powder.

Add plaster as instructed before and mix well to make sure the colour is evenly dispersed.

CASTING

A plaster cast is made using a mould. This is a negative impression of an original (the positive). There are many different types of mould but the casting technique is the same for all. Wet plaster is poured into the mould and is left to go off; the cast (set plaster) is then removed. Some moulds can be used over and over again, but in this section we look at taking casts from moulds which are discarded after use.

Ready-made moulds
A wide variety of ready-made moulds come to us in the form of packaging – for example, yoghurt pots and the clear hard plastic shapes used to hold items in place on display cards. Look out for these – you will be amazed by the plethora of interesting shapes you can cast from them. They are useful for experimenting with different decorative finishes – or you may even cast an interesting object in its own right!

To determine how much plaster to mix, fill the mould with water and then pour the water into the mixing bowl. Make up your mix of plaster as described on page 10.

Pour in the plaster slowly and evenly until the mould is half full. Let the plaster settle and then gently shake the mould from side to side to ensure that you get an even distribution.

Fill the mould with plaster. If you pour in too much plaster, use a spatula to level off the top. Hold the mould firmly and gently agitate to expel any air bubbles.

When dry carefully remove the cast from the mould. If necessary, cut the flange with scissors and peel the plastic from the cast.

Use sandpaper to smooth away rough edges.

Tip You may need to support the mould to keep it level if it is an awkward shape. Use lumps of Plasticine or pieces of wood where necessary. Always replace the mould onto its support carefully after agitating the mix to expel air bubbles.

Press moulds

You can push all sorts of objects into a thick bed of clay or Plasticine and pour plaster into the negative spaces.

Knead the Plasticine to soften it. Roll out a thick slab.

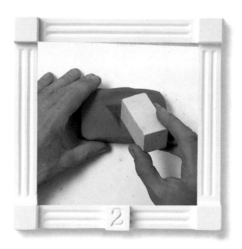

Coat your object with washing-up liquid to prevent it sticking. Push it into the Plasticine.

Build a wall around the impression with strips of Plasticine. Use a modelling tool to blend where the wall joins the base to ensure an effective seal, both inside and out.

Take a cast. Release it by peeling away the Plasticine.

LATEX MOULDS

Latex is a flexible mould-making material which picks up fine surface detail from a positive. Here we demonstrate how to make a one-piece mould which will peel off easily. Once it has been made – and it is straightforward to do – multiple casts can be taken which opens up the possibilities for making and decorating.

Laying on the coats

A latex mould is made by painting on latex. The first coats are quite liquid so fine detail can be seeked out. The following coats have thickener added so both strength and thickness can be built up. However, if too much thickener is added the mould will not be as flexible. Use an old brush because if the latex sets on the bristles it will be ruined. Between applying coats keep your brush in the pot of latex to stop it drying out, and be quick to wash brushes in hot soapy water when you have finished. Keep the lid firmly on the latex pot to avoid a skin forming.

Undercuts

Undercuts (gaps between the object and the baseboard on which it rests) allow latex to flow underneath and thus prevent the easy removal of a mould. Latex is a very flexible material and is able to stretch over minor undercuts but it is important to reduce them to a minimum. Before starting to make a mould, fill any undercuts with Plasticine.

The support jacket

Latex is a flexible material and therefore needs support. When a cast is taken the mould is held firm by a specially made plaster support jacket. It prevents distortion when the plaster is poured in and ensures the plaster surface sets level.

Building a wall

Roll out a thick slab of Plasticine or modelling clay and cut it into strips: the width should be the depth of the positive (the object you have made a mould from) at its highest point plus 1in (2.5cm). Position these to make a wall approximately 1in (2.5cm) from the positive and smooth the clay into the baseboard to make a tight seal.

A latex fish mould

This example uses the fish relief (see page 82). Any undercuts should be filled with Plasticine.

Paint the first coat of latex onto the fish and onto the baseboard to make a flange all the way around. Leave to dry. Paint on another five coats of latex, allowing each to dry before applying the next.

Make up a mix of latex and latex thickener and paint on three coats, again allowing each to dry in between.

Build a wall of Plasticine around the fish at the outer edge of the latex flange.

Pour the plaster in slowly and evenly; rushing may result in a collapsed wall. Tap the baseboard to expel any air bubbles.

When the plaster has gone off remove the Plasticine wall and gently slide the whole unit off the baseboard. Turn it over.

Hold the latex flange and gently pull the fish out of its plaster case. The latex is quite strong and very flexible so it can be pulled and stretched.

Peel off the latex mould and wash it in soapy water. Replace the mould in the plaster case.

Tip Integrate hanging hooks as part of the casting process to ensure a strong fixing. Bend a piece of wire and hang it in the plaster from a length of dowelling which rests on either edge of the support jacket.

CARE AND REPAIR

16

No matter how careful you are accidents will happen and plaster objects are especially vulnerable to breakages. However, if a plaster cast does break or get damaged do not despair – everything is repairable. Two techniques are shown here which can be used to repair any plaster object. If the broken fragment is available it is straightforward; otherwise plaster is modelled to the required shape.

Superglue

The simplest method of repairing cracks and broken fragments is to use superglue.

Push the head onto the neck and hold it in place and at the same time wipe off any excess glue with a damp cloth.

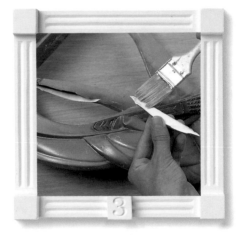

Wet the exposed areas of plaster on both the object and the fragment which has broken off.

Squeeze some superglue onto the fragment and push it into place. Hold firmly in position for a few seconds until the glue has set.

Wet the crack by pushing in a wet brush. Hold the tube above the crack and gently squeeze so the glue falls into the crack.

Health and safety

- Always wear barrier cream and rubber gloves when working with plaster and latex as they can be skin irritants; use soapy water to wash any areas of the body which come into contact with them.

- A dust mask may be worn if the air becomes filled with plaster dust.

- Work in well-ventilated areas to avoid fumes from latex and spray paints.

- Take great care when using scalpels and metal cutters, cutting away from the body; never cut towards yourself.

Applying new plaster

Broken fragments can easily be lost or they may be shattered into tiny pieces. In this case, you must repair your object by applying layers of new plaster. The exposed plaster on the ornament needs to be thoroughly wetted with water before applying new plaster. Otherwise, the plaster on the ornament will draw out the water from the newly applied plaster and it will not go off properly. Use a softer type of plaster for repair work as it is easier to form into the required shape once it has gone off.

Make a mix of plaster and leave it to thicken. Use a brush to lay it on around the wire. Keep building up the thickness of plaster in this way.

Sand the repair to the necessary shape, blending it in with the overall shape. This can now be painted to finish the repair.

This ornament has a wire support embedded in the plaster and new plaster is built up around this. Wet the exposed areas of plaster.

When you have built up the shape, use a wet brush to level the repair with the surrounding surface. Leave to dry.

ANIMAL KINGDOM

The use of a paper template is an easy way to model clay or Plasticine shapes in relief. This technique is used to model the Chameleon Clock and the Farm Animals. Once you have mastered this technique you can carry on to make all manner of animals, or indeed any relief shape. The Teddy Bear is cast from a bought mould and is painted with great precision to show its finely modelled forms and surface to best effect. The Vatican Lions are plaster blanks and their surfaces are treated to give the impression of prolonged exposure to the elements.

Miniature versions of the lions to be seen outside the Vatican in Rome can be finished to resemble the weathered colour of the originals. The sandstone and lichen surface is replicated by applying acrylic paint using different techniques and building up the colour in stages. Placed either side of a doorway they will exude a magnificence despite their smaller scale.

VATICAN LIONS

Dip a paintbrush into some white paint and then brush it out on some paper, leaving the brush relatively dry. Drag it across the surface so paint is picked up on the high points.

MATERIALS

Plaster lions
Acrylic paint:
yellow ochre,
white, raw sienna
and emerald green
Copper paint
Green patina paint

EQUIPMENT

Small palette
Paintbrushes
Toothbrush
Wide mesh
cloth/natural
sponge

Apply yellow ochre paint to the whole lion, creating an opaque surface. Leave to dry.

Using raw sienna paint repeat the technique to obtain a dry brush. Hold the brush vertically and dab it to achieve a stippled effect. An uneven application will look more natural.

Apply more white paint unevenly using an open weave cloth. Gradually build the paint up over the whole surface.

There are many metallic paints available which produce extremely realistic results. This lion has been painted copper using a paint that contains ground metal. If you wish to achieve a weathered look, apply a coat of green patina paint while the second coat of copper is still tacky.

Mix some watery green paint and use a toothbrush to spatter it over the whole surface. Repeat the effect with watery yellow ochre paint.

This free standing pig is made starting with a simple drawing of a pig – children's illustrated books are a good source of inspiration. The pig is formed in modelling clay, from which a latex mould is made. The plaster cast is painted in bright colours in keeping with its highly stylized form. It can be a lone pig or it could be the first of a farmyard set.

FARM ANIMALS

MATERIALS

Modelling clay
Copper wire
Copper sheet
Plaster
Latex
Acrylic paint: red,
yellow, green, blue,
white and black
Gold powder
Cellulose varnish
Dowelling wood

EQUIPMENT

Rolling pin
Baseboard
Modelling tools
Felt tip pen
Small pointed pliers
Mixing bowl
Sandpaper
Paintbrushes
Small mixing dish

Roll out a ¾in (19mm) thick slab of clay.

Lay a copy of the template provided on top of the clay. Using a modelling tool, cut through the clay, carefully following the outline of the template.

Keep the template on top of the clay and use a modelling tool to trace the drawn lines to produce indentations on the clay's surface.

Wet the clay and use a wide-ended modelling tool to press the clay down at an angle to follow the form of the body as it rises up and away from the leg.

Use a combination of modelling
tools and your fingers on the wet
clay to develop the pig's form
using the indentations on the
clay's surface as guidelines.

When the modelling is complete
you are ready to make a latex
mould (see page 14).

Use pliers to form a spiral of
copper wire for the tail. Bend
the wire at right angles to this
and bend again as shown.

When you cast the pig
incorporate the tail by suspending
it from a skewer resting on either
side of the mould.

Smooth the edges of the cast
with sandpaper. You are now
ready to paint your pig.

Photocopy this template or
draw your own design.

24

Mix red and white paint to produce pink and cover the whole surface of the pig.

While the paint is still wet brush some red paint into the crevices where the body meets the legs and blend in. Blend red paint over the whole surface to achieve a variety of pink tones.

Mix black and white paint together and apply grey patches over the pig's body. When dry, paint with cellulose varnish.

Paint white onto the legs, nose and ears.

14

To make a cockscomb, cut out a triangle from a sheet of copper. Make a series of parallel cuts along one edge to produce a comb-like effect.

Make a cow from a thick layer of clay and sandpaper the bottom of the legs so that it is freestanding. By adding a stick to the cockerel it can be used to adorn plant pots.

26 This teddy bear was cast into plaster from a purchased rubber mould. It was meticulously modelled and the cast is decorated with equal precision. Because more than one teddy bear can be cast you can make several, each unique with different colour combinations. This project is a good exercise in painting fine detailed surfaces, for which you need a very steady hand.

TEDDY BEAR

Use a cardboard box with a hole cut in the lid to suspend the mould.

Paint a very watery mix of burnt sienna over the base coat so the colour sinks into the crevices. Avoid making drip marks.

MATERIALS

Rubber mould
Plaster
Acrylic paint:
Naples yellow,
burnt sienna,
yellow, green,
white, black, red
and blue

EQUIPMENT

Small mixing dish
Paintbrush
Mixing bowl

Paint a thin base coat of Naples yellow over the bear's body and allow to dry.

Paint the waistcoat yellow. Dip your brush into the yellow paint, dry most of it off with a rag and then brush across the body so the high points of the surface pick up the paint.

Add white to yellow to make a light tone and paint the nose, paws, eyes and the inside of the ears. Carefully paint vertical stripes on the waistcoat.

Paint the eyes with burnt sienna; paint the star on the ball with Naples yellow and the circles red. Finally, carefully paint a blue stripe around the ball.

This teddy bear has black fur and a bright red waistcoat. The striking colours produce a very different effect from that of the brown bear.

28

Change is the theme of this clock – the time is constantly changing and the chameleon changes the colour of its skin. The clock face is sculpted in modelling clay with the aid of templates and cast into plaster using a latex mould. The battery-driven clock mechanism, which has an integral hanging hook, is easily obtained and fits to the back of the clock face.

Draw your design of the clock face on paper using the chameleon template provided.

CHAMELEON CLOCK

MATERIALS

Paper
Modelling clay
Plaster
Latex
Acrylic paint:
green, yellow and
blue
Gold powder
Cellulose varnish
Clock mechanism

EQUIPMENT

Rolling pin
Modelling tools
Felt tip pen
Mixing bowl
Sandpaper
Palette
Baseboard

Roll out some modelling clay on the baseboard to a thickness of ¾in (19mm).

Lay the clock face template on top of the clay and cut round it with a modelling tool. Cut out an extra chameleon using the template provided.

Keep the templates on top of the clay and use a modelling tool to trace the drawn lines to produce indentations on the clay's surface. Mark the centre point of the clock face.

Place a modelling tool vertically on the centre mark and rotate it to enlarge the hole.

Use the sharp end of a modelling tool to add contrasting textures to the body. Only slight pressure is needed to produce such marks.

Place the cut out chameleon on top of one of the chameleons on the clock face. Use a modelling tool to blend the clay along the cut edges of these two sections. This end will be the top of the clock.

Wet the surface of the clay and, using the indentations as guidelines, start to model the chameleon form. A wet finger run over the surface helps to consolidate the shape.

Select a wide-ended modelling tool and run it around the inside rim of the clock face to produce a bevel, smoothing it out with wet fingers. Shape the other chameleon as before.

When the modelling is complete make a latex mould (see page 14) and take a plaster cast. Smooth the edges with sandpaper.

Paint yellow in the gaps between the turquoise. A touch of orange paint blended into the top of each yellow stripe gives an illusion of form. Paint the other chameleon in the same way.

Paint dark turquoise stripes on the chameleon. Note how they do not follow the direction of the indented marks. When dry, paint parts of these stripes with a lighter colour turquoise.

Paint the clock face blue, using as many coats as necessary to obtain a thick even colour. Allow the paint to dry between coats.

Paint the circumference of the clock mauve and fill in the areas not already painted blue. When the paint has dried turn the clock over and paint the back blue.

Working in a well-ventilated area, paint the whole of the clock, back and front, with a coat of cellulose varnish.

Mix some gold powder and
varnish to a creamy consistency
and paint a decorative border
around the clock.

To fit the clock mechanism push
the central spindle through the
hole in the centre and screw
down the hands.

MARK LA TROBE
Egyptian cats
The marbled effect was achieved by adding a water-based dye to the plaster. The dye was not mixed fully into the plaster but folded in loosely.

MARK LA TROBE • Three shelves
Staining with diluted furniture wax produces the effect of old plaster, from a dark oak colour to the off white of clear wax.

MARK LA TROBE
Wise owl
Holes were drilled so that large glass eyes could be securely glued in place. Used on a slow setting, drilling will not break plaster casts.

GALLERY

Animals have inspired artists throughout the ages; here we see cats rendered in plaster in the Egyptian tradition. Animals have also been used to adorn buildings and fountains, as exemplified by the griffin and lion heads. Whether purely ornamental, like the majestic lounging lion, the wise owl and the cockerel wall plaques, or cast as utilitarian bookends, animals make a dramatic decorative statement.

MARK LA TROBE
Dog bookends
Meticulously modelled and stained with diluted furniture wax, these dogs are difficult for the beginner to sculpt but a simpler version is within everybody's capabilities.

PAMELA STEWART-PEARSON
Two cockerels
A wood carving was the original for these reliefs. They were painted with acrylic paint with gilded wax applied on top.

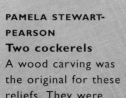

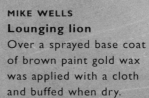

MIKE WELLS
Lounging lion
Over a sprayed base coat of brown paint gold wax was applied with a cloth and buffed when dry.

◄▼ BERNARD CLAYDON
Griffin and lion's head
The original figures were modelled in clay, from which silicone rubber moulds were made. The turquoise and verdigris colourings were achieved by using an airbrush.

MARK LA TROBE
Lion's head
This cast is based on a fountain head design and is an example of the many pieces of classical sculpture which are now available as plaster casts.

Painting the plaster cast as naturalistically as possible is the order of the day in this chapter. The press mould technique is used to make an attractive Mini-veg Panel. A latex mould is made of one side of a fossil, a plaster cast taken and this is then coloured to replicate the surface of the original. Platicine is modelled freehand to make the Sunflower Candle Holder and Plant Pot Stick; the plaster casts are painted with bright colours to reflect the ambience of their inspiration. Bought rubber moulds are used to cast different fruits which are

ORGANIC ORIGINS

painted in a way that will convince the eye but unfortunately not your teeth! Blending paint together is further explored when decorating the blank plaster swag; this is also shown with a metallic finish to demonstrate the various effects you can achieve.

A latex mould was made from a found object – a fossil – and then cast into plaster. As it is a one-piece mould you must choose the best side of the fossil to work from. In this project we replicate the surface colouring of the original fossil as closely as possible. The finished fossil makes an attractive ornament or a useful paperweight.

FOSSIL

Granite spray paints are widely available. This fossil was sprayed blue granite and the crevices emphasized with black paint.

You are now ready to make a latex mould (see page 14) and take a cast.

MATERIALS

Fossil
Plasticine
Plaster
Latex
Acrylic paint: black, white and yellow
Whiting powder
Blue granite spray paint

EQUIPMENT

Mixing bowl
Paintbrush
Toothbrush
Sponge
Small mixing dish
Baseboard

Fill in the undercuts of the fossil with Plasticine and build halfway up the fossil.

Mix white and black acrylic paint to produce a mid-tone grey and cover the surface of the plaster cast. Leave to dry.

Dab black acrylic paint onto the surface with a sponge. Use a ragged rather than a straight edge of the sponge.

Brush on a coat of watery yellow paint and while wet use a sponge to dab whiting powder on top. Leave to dry.

Remove the excess whiting with a damp sponge.

Make a watery mix of light grey. Use a toothbrush to spatter the paint onto the surface. Leave to dry.

40

A plaster blank of ribbons, fruit and flowers – known as a swag – is painted to produce a brightly coloured decorative element. It looks good on its own or several can be joined to make a chain of swags to sweep across a wall. The naturalistic sunflower head could be incorporated with other elements to make an alternative type of swag.

FLOWER SWAGS

MATERIALS

Plaster swag
Plaster sunflower
Acrylic paint:
green, crimson,
yellow, blue, brown
and white
Bronze paint
Ruby red metallic
paint

EQUIPMENT

Palette
Paintbrush

Paint the individual elements systematically, using the same colour for each type.

Use bright colours to paint the individual elements of the swag. Dark orange was painted over a lighter orange and then blended in.

As more and more elements of the swag are painted the colours intensify as they contrast with or complement each other.

Bright red bows at either end of the swag provide a strong compositional device for this multicoloured decoration.

Add white to the tip of each petal and blend in to produce a gradation of tone running from top to bottom. Paint the centre brown. Pick out the high points with white and blend in.

Over a bronze base coat apply metallic ruby red paint using a dry brush so that only the high points pick up the paint.

Mix green and white and paint the leaves. Paint a darker green in the crevices and a touch of white on the tip of each leaf. Paint the petals yellow.

42 Fruit have remained a popular subject for artists for centuries. In this project plaster casts of a pear, orange and apple are made from bought moulds and then painted using acrylic paints. To obtain a naturalistic look a variety of shades of colour should be applied to each fruit and blended in. It is a good opportunity to practise colour mixing. While painting it is helpful to have a selection of fruit to refer to.

FRUIT

MATERIALS

Rubber moulds
Plaster
Acrylic paint:
green, yellow, blue,
red and white
Cellulose varnish

EQUIPMENT

Mixing bowl
Small mixing dish
Paintbrush

Mix a base coat for the pear from green and yellow paint. Leave to dry.

Paint on different shades of green: add blue to darken the green or yellow to lighten it.

Cover the surface with patches of various shades to recreate the surface of a pear.

Paint the surface of the pear with cellulose varnish. Use even strokes and avoid drip marks.

Paint the other fruits in a similar way: the base colour for the orange is a mixture of red and yellow; red for the apple. Blend white highlights into the fruit and darker lowlights. Paint both with cellulose varnish.

Instead of using cellulose varnish, apply an oil-based varnish such as Japan gold size and then a coat of gum arabic. This will produce a crackle glaze.

44

A sunflower is modelled from Plasticine using a variety of modelling tools. A latex mould is then made from which multiple casts can be taken – each can be decorated in different ways. The candle holder makes a good table decoration and the plant pot stick is an unusual feature for a flower pot – it adds dazzle when a plant is not flowering.

SUNFLOWERS

MATERIALS

Plasticine
Latex
Plaster
Acrylic paint:
Turner's yellow,
cadmium yellow,
cadmium red, blue,
green and white
Dowelling wood

EQUIPMENT

Baseboard
Modelling tool
Rolling pin
Mixing bowl
Paintbrush
Small mixing dish
Film cannister

Shape a piece of Plasticine into a basic leaf shape and curl one end under. Use a modelling tool to draw the veins. Attach this to the central element securely.

Knead the Plasticine and make a semi-spherical shape. Push a plastic film cannister into the centre to make a socket for the candle. Any object with the correct diameter can be used.

Roll a ball of Plasticine, pinch one of the edges and tease it out to make a petal. Arrange petals all around the central element, attaching them securely.

Blend the Plasticine seams. With a pointed modelling tool make holes in the central area.

Take plaster casts from your moulds. Mix Turner's yellow and cadmium yellow with a touch of red and paint the petals of both of the sunflowers.

Apply green paint to the leaf and the dowelling. Mix brown by adding blue and red to the yellow and paint the flower centres. Paint white on the high points and a darker yellow on the low points of the petals, and a lighter green on the leaf.

Model a smaller sunflower using simpler shapes but no large leaf. Use dowelling to create a cavity for a stick to be attached when it has been cast into plaster. Now make a latex mould of each flower (see page 14).

46 This attractive wall panel is made by casting small varieties of vegetables into plaster using the press mould technique. Plasticine is wrapped around each vegetable to make a negative of its form and pick up surface detail. If the Plasticine moulds are handled carefully they can be reused many times.

MINI-VEG PANEL

MATERIALS

Plasticine
Plaster
Scrim
Mini vegetables
Vegetable oil
Acrylic paint
Gloss and matt
varnish
Galvanized wire

EQUIPMENT

Kitchen knife
Scissors
Baseboard
Strips of timber
2in (5cm) oval nails
Rolling pin
Paintbrush
Mixing bowl
Palette

Trim the Plasticine level where it meets. Carefully open out the Plasticine just enough to remove the sweetcorn. Return the Plasticine to its original form.

Brush a coat of vegetable oil inside the mould and fill with plaster. When it has gone off gently peel back the Plasticine to remove the cast. Repeat this process for the other vegetables.

Roll out a slab of Plasticine about ½in (13mm) thick, and push the sweetcorn into its surface. Fold the Plasticine around its form, pressing well.

Make a frame to fit around the baseboard. Tack the frame together with nails – the frame needs to be easily dismantled. Seal the gaps between baseboard and frame with Plasticine.

Pour plaster into the frame. While the plaster is still wet lay the scrim on top. Gently push it slightly below the surface.

Remove the plaster panel by dismantling the frame. Arrange the vegetable casts on the panel in a pleasing composition and then draw around each.

Cut some scrim slightly smaller than the area inside the frame. Coat the baseboard and the inside surfaces of the frame with vegetable oil.

Bend two pieces of wire to make hanging hooks. Place them in the wet plaster, carefully lifting up the scrim to slip the two curled sections underneath. Rest the circular parts on the frame.

Use a kitchen knife to score the underside of each vegetable cast and its corresponding position on the panel. This will ensure a good fixing.

Mix a small quantity of plaster and when it has thickened to a cream cheese consistency apply it to a scored area on the panel. Press the cast on top of it. Repeat to adhere all the casts.

Brush wet plaster along the plaster join between the casts and the panel. Leave to dry thoroughly.

Paint carrots orange. Paint red and white rings across them to give the impression of indentations and highlights.

Paint tomatoes and chillies a deep red. Paint sweetcorn yellow; when dry lightly brush white paint onto the high points.

Use a modelling tool to trim off the excess plaster which squeezed out between the casts and the panel.

Paint the background to resemble wood grain. Apply a variety of browns in long continuous strokes across the board. Add a couple of circular wood knots.

Paint the stalks of chillies green and the leaves of cauliflowers in two shades of green, keeping the stalky parts of the leaf a lighter green than the rest.

Apply matt varnish to the board and vegetables such as okra and gloss varnish to vegetables such as tomatoes.

Paint okra the same shades of green but blend the colours well and paint the high points with a dark green. Use vertical brushstrokes in varying shades of brown and red for onions.

THE WORKS • Rock mirror
The original form for this mirror was made using real pebbles and the plaster cast replicates their texture.

SARAH WILLIAMS • Spiral wall plaque
The rich colours used in medieval manuscripts and images from folk art inspired the design of this relief. It was painted with acrylic paint and gold leaf.

GALLERY

The organic world provides a wealth of inspiration. The rock mirror is an excellent example of using actual organic objects as the starting point for a plasterwork. It is interesting to see how the two leaf mirrors each display a different facet of the leaf shape. The brightly coloured plaque uses a spiral as its central motif, an abstract representation of the cycles of nature. Fruit and flowers are used imaginatively and to great effect in the other plasterworks.

MARK LA TROBE • Swag, fruitbowl and wreath
These wall plaques were modelled in clay from which silicone rubber moulds were made. The subsequent plaster casts have light coloured wax applied to them; when dry the wax was buffed to produce a surface shine.

THE WORKS
Leaf mirror
The mirror surround was painted with cobalt blue and then coats of gilt cream were brushed on daily. It was then varnished.

INTERIOR DESIGNS

There is an abundance of blank plaster casts available for decoration. A lot if not most of these are based on traditional classical designs, such as the Column. The Column has been chosen to demonstrate the most complex decorative technique in this book: marbling. The Uplighter, although of a classical design, allows you to attach an electric light fitting to it; this is given an antiqued finish. The traditional Fleur-de-Lys is here modelled in Plasticine and a variety of coloured casts are taken from the latex mould. The picture frame and bows are decorated with bright flat colours in a variety of striking designs. The Rosettes are stained with powder paint and coated with a textured gel which belies the smooth surface of the plaster cast.

Show off your favourite photograph or picture in this highly decorative picture frame. Acrylic paint is used and sealed with cellulose varnish. All the colours can be found using only the primary colours – red, blue and yellow – together with white. The painted surface is then highlighted with gold.

GOTHIC FRAME

When you paint the very deep red you will need to have a steady hand to avoid brushing paint onto areas that have already been painted.

MATERIALS

Plaster picture
frame
Acrylic paints:
yellow, red, blue
and white
Gold powder
Cellulose varnish

EQUIPMENT

Small paintbrush
Palette
Small mixing dish

Follow the colour scheme shown, starting with yellow paint. Then paint the turquoise and mauve areas. It does not matter if you go over the edges at this point.

Paint the remaining areas of the frame with a dark blue, including the back. Paint evenly and avoid leaving brush marks. If the coat is too streaked, repaint when dry.

In a small mixing bowl mix some varnish and gold powder to a creamy consistency. Use a paintbrush to highlight details.

Leave to dry completely. In a well-ventilated area seal the entire frame with a coat of clear cellulose varnish.

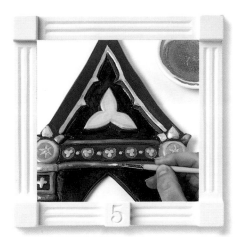

Brush off the excess paint on a sheet of paper until the brush is relatively dry. Drag it lightly across the surface of the frame to leave a light deposit.

Use superglue to stick the glass and hanging hook onto the back. Place the picture face down on the glass with a piece of card on top and secure them in position with tape.

58

There are many plaster casts of architectural features available ready to be decorated and used for interior decoration. The finish on the uplighter gives the impression that it is an old architectural feature. Rosettes look effective on cornicing around the top of a wall or the architrave around a door. The textured finish shown here belies the smooth surface of plaster.

UPLIGHTER AND ROSETTES

Rub off excess wax with a cloth. Leave the wax to dry.

MATERIALS

Plaster uplighter
Plaster rosettes
Antique wax
furniture polish
White spirit
Textured acrylic gel
Acrylic paint:
bronze yellow,
Naples yellow,
burnt umber,
black and white
Blue and red
powder paint

EQUIPMENT

Small jar
Paintbrushes
Soft cloth
Small mixing dish

Dilute antique wax with white spirit to make it liquid enough to apply with a paintbrush. Brush it onto the plaster, taking care to avoid drip marks.

Use a soft cloth to buff the whole of the uplighter to produce an aged-looking surface.

Apply textured acrylic gel evenly over the surface of a rosette. Mix bronze yellow with Naples yellow and apply a base coat. Paint on a wash of darker tone.

Stipple on burnt umber, reaching into the crevices. Before the paint dries soften the edges with a dry brush. Repeat this technique using grey paint. Apply creamy yellow paint to the high points using a dry brush.

Dampen the rosette and sprinkle it with coloured powder paint. Brush off the excess powder after ten minutes. The dampened plaster will absorb some of the colour.

60

The traditional image of the fleur-de-lys was originally found in architecture but has been adopted by Western culture – for instance, it is used on flags, coats of arms, fabric designs etc. Its relief format makes it an ideal shape for casting from a latex mould. Coloured plaster is used for the cast and then a metallic finish is applied.

FLEUR-DE-LYS

MATERIALS

Plasticine
Latex
Plaster
Red, green and blue
powder paint
Silver and gold
acrylic paint or wax
White spirit

EQUIPMENT

Pencil
Modelling tools
Paintbrush
Mixing bowl
Baseboard
Small mixing dish

Make a copy of the template provided. Place it on the board and draw round it.

Build up the forms inside the drawn lines with Plasticine. Use a modelling tool to keep the Plasticine hard against the lines.

Continue to model the form, applying the Plasticine with your fingers and defining the shape with a modelling tool.

With the basic form of the fleur-de-lys filled in, use the blade of a wide-ended modelling tool to slice the excess Plasticine off the main form to create a smooth angular surface. Use a smaller tool to define the more detailed areas of the form.

Dip a finger in white spirit and run it over the surface of the form to produce a smooth surface. You are now ready to make a latex mould (see page 14). Cast the fleur-de-lys using blue, green and red coloured plaster (see page 11).

Finish the blue plaster cast by painting the side elements with silver paint. Finish the red fleur-de-lys by painting the central element with gold paint. Apply gold paint to one of the bevelled sides of each element of the green cast.

62

Ribbons and bows are available in many different styles and can be used as individual decorative elements or to frame other plasterworks such as a swag. Here, they are shown with a bold scarlet finish, in softer blue and yellow colours, and in a striking tartan.

RIBBONS AND BOWS

This tartan has thick ultramarine stripes with thin pairs of black stripes in between.

MATERIALS

Plaster bows
Acrylic paint: blue, purple, crimson, ultramarine, black, yellow and hooker's green

EQUIPMENT

Paintbrush
Small mixing dish

Apply a base coat of hooker's green. Work out your tartan design. The important thing is to paint the stripes in regular, repeating patterns.

The final touch is made by mixing a small amount of green with yellow and painting a pattern of light stripes on the bow.

Paint this ribbon yellow on top and blue on the underside. Follow the flow of the bow as you apply the yellow. Paint the crevices on the knot with brown.

Paint crimson over the whole surface and allow to dry. Brush purple into the crevices and the high points of the knot.

Paint the underside of the ribbon light blue.

64

Time and patience is required to achieve this marble effect. Before you start, familiarize yourself with the various colourings and patterns of different types of marble – look at marble floors and walls of buildings and sculpture and plinths in museums. Note pattern details which interest you and make a drawing of your proposed decoration.

MARBLED COLUMN

Use a cloth to apply scumble glaze over the entire surface of the column: when paint is applied it will stay wet longer, allowing it to be manipulated to achieve the desired effect.

MATERIALS

Plaster column
White eggshell paint
Fine wet and dry sandpaper
Scumble glaze
Oil paint: burnt sienna, raw sienna, chrome yellow, Indian red, white and ultramarine
White spirit
Satin varnish
Beeswax

EQUIPMENT

Paintbrushes
Hog bristle brush
Badgerhair brush
Sable brush (No 1)
Dusting brush
Feather
Rag
Newspaper
Soft cloth

Seal the column by painting on two coats of eggshell paint, allowing the first coat to dry before applying the second. When dry smooth the surface with wet and dry sandpaper. Clean with a dusting brush.

Dilute burnt sienna oil paint with white spirit to produce a very thin wash and brush on quickly. Follow this with a thin wash of raw sienna.

While the paint is still wet, stipple with a hog bristle brush to soften the surface. With a badgerhair brush lightly stroke the paint surface in all directions to remove the brush marks.

Soak some screwed up newspaper in white spirit and dab it on: this will break up the paint surface. Use the badgerhair brush to soften this.

Mix burnt sienna with chrome yellow paint and make a thin wash. Stipple it onto the base of the column, then with a hog bristle brush blend in by stippling in all directions. This dark tone will give the base of the column some visual weight.

Before you begin marbling, make a drawing of the column and its proposed decoration to refer to.

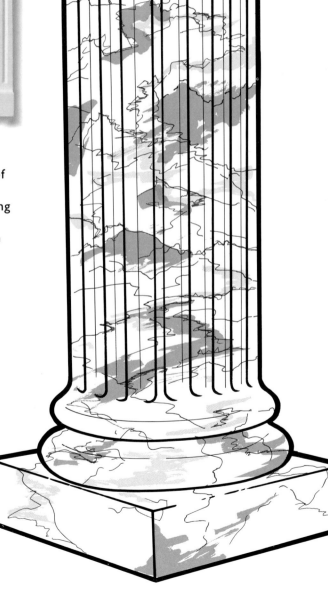

Mix Indian red, burnt sienna and a touch of ultramarine with white spirit and a dab of scumble glaze. Use a sable brush to add veins between the light and dark areas.

Stipple the veins with the hog bristle brush and then soften them with the badgerhair brush, following the direction of the veins. Add more veins.

For variety, charge your brush with ultramarine on one side and a mixture of raw and burnt sienna on the other. Dilute the colours more to obtain a lighter tone for these secondary veins.

Following the course of the large veins, paint fine veins in a predominantly blue tone mixed from burnt sienna and ultramarine. Stipple and soften with the hog bristle and badgerhair brushes.

Damp a rag with white spirit and wipe off areas of the base colour – large and small – around the veins to reveal the white plaster.

Dip a feather in a thin wash of white oil paint and drag it across the surface using a jittery motion. This produces a very subtle effect.

Paint the whole of the column with a wash of raw sienna. Stipple and soften with a hog bristle and badgerhair brush as before and allow to dry. Coat with satin varnish.

A final polish with beeswax enhances all the colours and hides any remaining brushstrokes.

GALLERY

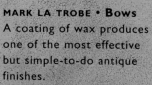

MARK LA TROBE • Bows
A coating of wax produces
one of the most effective
but simple-to-do antique
finishes.

◄ FUNKY ECLECTICA
Pewter mirror
Art Nouveau designs were the inspiration for this mirror. The original was made in wood and gesso, from which a silicone mould was made. Silver and bronze powders were used for the finish.

Plaster has long been used as a building material and the different periods in history provide a wide range of architectural designs for us to draw upon. The capital, rosette and shelf are directly derived from classical originals; the bows are traditional decorations but have a more modern feel to them; Art Nouveau inspired one of the mirrors while old church carvings inspired the other; Gothic and Baroque traditions inspired the box and small plaques.

▲► CLIFTON LITTLE VENICE
Soane rosette and ionic capital
Cast in lightly coloured and plain white plaster, these classic architectural features can transform a room.

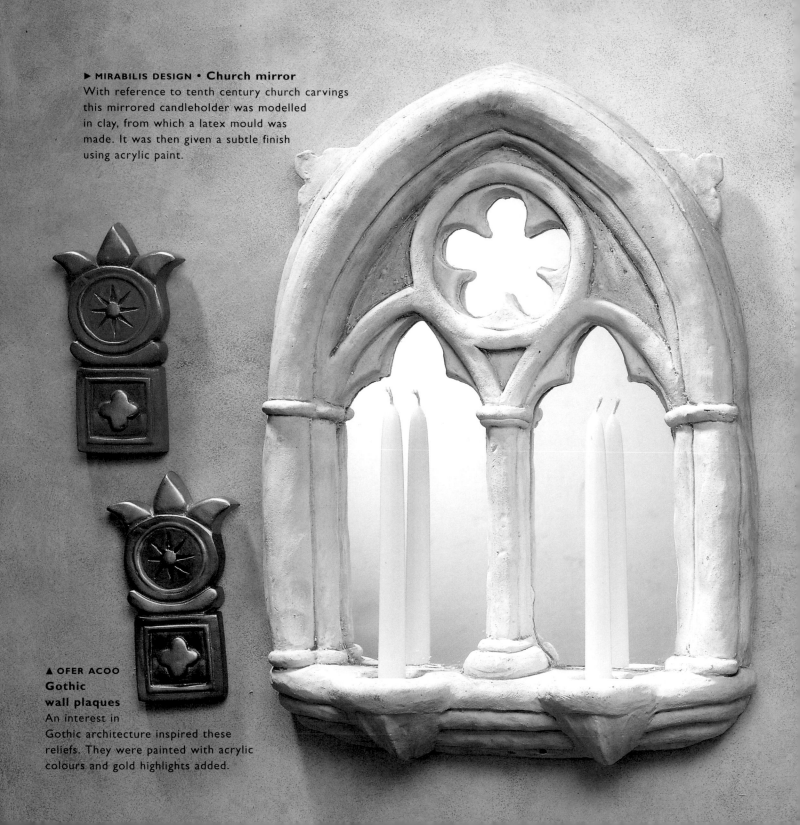

▶ **MIRABILIS DESIGN • Church mirror**
With reference to tenth century church carvings
this mirrored candleholder was modelled
in clay, from which a latex mould was
made. It was then given a subtle finish
using acrylic paint.

▲ **OFER ACOO**
Gothic
wall plaques
An interest in
Gothic architecture inspired these
reliefs. They were painted with acrylic
colours and gold highlights added.

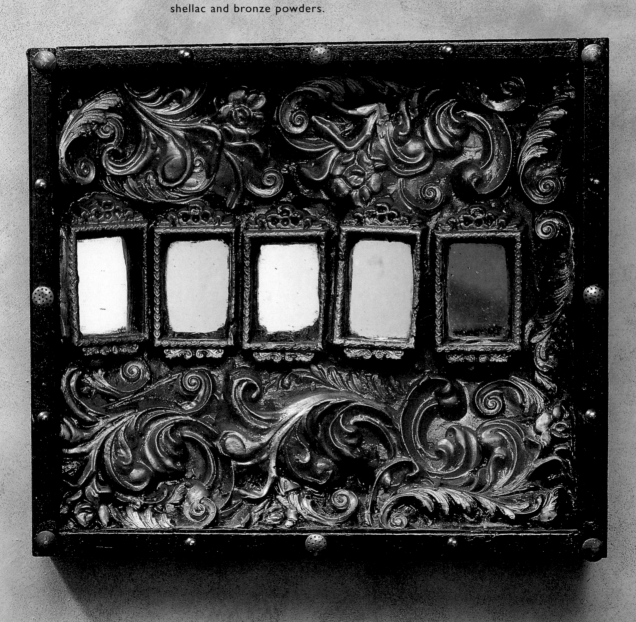

FUNKY ECLECTICA • Blue baroque box
The artist modelled this relief in clay and cast
it into plaster using a one-off mould. Its rich
decorative finish was produced using tinted
shellac and bronze powders.

OCEAN WORLD

The paint effects used in this chapter seek to emulate the glistening and shimmering effect of water and its associated sea objects. The Starfish and Scallop come as plaster blanks and are decorated with pearlized paint. The paint effects used on the Shell Tiles also invoke that sense of the sea, albeit with one of the tiles being decorated using a teabag! The Sculpted Shell and the Tropical Fish are modelled with different surface textures which show how effectively a latex mould picks up detail. The Jumping Fish is cast from a bought mould and decorated with layers of washes which emulate the fish's scales.

The starfish and scallop shell shown here are decorated in complementary colours enrichened with pearlized paint and glitter. Both shapes have a flat back: a hanging hook can be glued to the back to hang them on a wall or they can simply be left as they are and placed on a shelf. Alternatively, you can decorate a few of each shape and arrange them as a frieze.

STARFISH AND SCALLOP

Fill the indentations on the high points with pearl white paint.

MATERIALS

Plaster starfish
Plaster scallop
Acrylic paint: blue, yellow, red and white
Pearl white paint
Blue glitter gel
Gold wax

EQUIPMENT

Paintbrush
Small mixing dish
Cloth

Mix a deep orange and paint a generous coat onto the whole surface of the starfish.

On a surface painted with pink pearlized paint, wipe gold wax lightly. Buff with a soft cloth when dry.

Paint the scallop shell blue and allow to dry. Rub a darker blue into this base coat.

Rub some blue glitter gel onto the surface and allow to dry.

Rub some gold wax onto the surface so that it reaches both the high points and the crevices.

Alternatively, apply turquoise pearlized paint and gold wax to pick out the ridges of the shell.

This fish relief was cast from a purchased rigid plastic mould and therefore did not need support while the plaster went off. It is decorated using acrylic paint. The colour on the main body is built up using washes (watery mixes of paint) and is effective in emulating fish scales.

JUMPING FISH

MATERIALS
———
Plastic mould
Plaster
Acrylic paint: blue,
yellow, lime green
and red
Cellulose varnish

EQUIPMENT
———
Mixing bowl
Small mixing dish
Paintbrush

Mix a green wash and paint the scales of the fish.

Mix an orange wash and paint the fins, gills and lips. Take care not to go over the edges onto the main body of the fish.

Paint dark red to pick out the detail on the fins.

Paint a wash of lime green over the scales to add highlights.

Apply a wash of blue randomly over the scales to break up the colour and add lowlights.

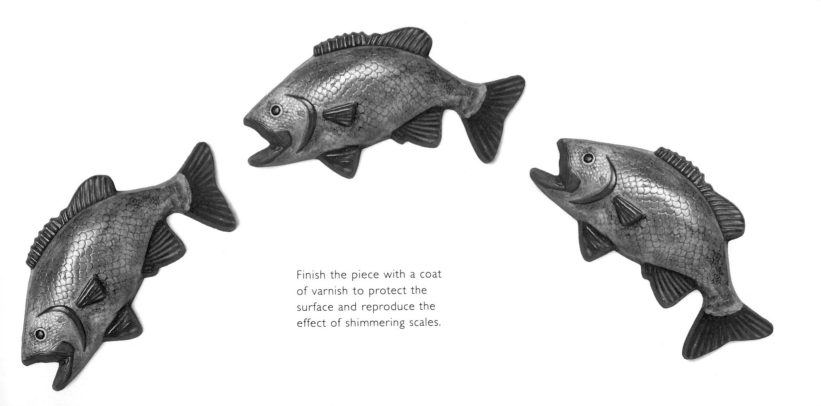

Finish the piece with a coat of varnish to protect the surface and reproduce the effect of shimmering scales.

A stylized shell is decorated to reflect glistening shells on a beach. First the shell is modelled in Plasticine as a relief, i.e. the underside is flat, making it suitable for a one-piece latex mould. Each plaster cast can be decorated using the same technique, changing the base colour for variety. When hanging in a cluster on a bathroom wall they exude a seaside flavour.

SCULPTED SHELL

MATERIALS

Plasticine
Latex
Plaster
Paperclip
Blue pearlized paint
Blue acrylic paint
Gold wax
Gold glitter

EQUIPMENT

Modelling tool
Paintbrushes
Cloth
Mixing bowl
Palette

Place the shape on your work surface and, applying light pressure, twist the form back and forth to create a flat back. Press the Plasticine with your fingers to create indentations to run around the shell from the opening to its tip.

Knead the Plasticine to make it pliable and model an elongated shell shape. Create an opening at one end with your fingers.

Roll out some very thin sausages of Plasticine and place them on the ridges. Use a modelling tool to make indentations on the surface.

You are now ready to make the latex mould (see page 14). When casting into plaster incorporate a hanging hook (see page 15).

Alternatively, paint the shell blue and sprinkle with gold glitter while still wet. Shake off the excess when dry.

Paint an even coat of pearlized blue paint all over the shell, taking care to avoid drip marks. Leave to dry.

When dry buff the shell with a soft cloth. The pearl in the paint and the gold will be enhanced when light falls on the shell.

Dip a cloth in gold wax and rub it lightly across the surface so that the colour is picked up by the high points of the shell.

80

These shell tiles can be interspersed with plain tiles on the walls of a bathroom. Pearlized paints produce a shimmering radiance; crackle glazing gives the impression of old paintings and hand-made crafts; staining with tea, plain or fruit flavoured, gives a more subtle and unusual effect. Tiles can be bought or made using the same method as for the mini-veg panel (see page 46).

SHELL TILES

While the paint is still wet use a brush loaded with white pearl paint to produce swirls of colour.

MATERIALS

Plaster tiles
Tea bag
Antique wax
furniture polish
White spirit
Oil-based varnish
(Japan gold size)
Gum arabic
Acrylic paint: blue,
pink and white
White pearl paint

EQUIPMENT

Small mixing dish
Paintbrushes
Small jar
Soft cloth

Brush a generous coat of light blue paint onto the background area of the tile.

Mix pink with pearl white, dilute to make a wash and apply to three of the shells. Mix blue with pearl white and apply to the remaining shells. Use water to blend in the background area.

Finish the shell in the same way as the uplighter (see page 58). Apply a coat of Japan gold size to the tile and allow to dry. Brush on a coat of gum arabic.

Apply blue paint on top: the paint will immediately crack and produce a rough, hand-painted effect. For a smoother look, apply the coat of paint first.

Pour hot water over a tea bag and dab it on the surface. Keep dipping the bag into the tea water to keep it moist and to freshen the tea colour.

82 Two methods of producing a relief are shown here. The fish relief is modelled direct in clay and provides the opportunity to experiment with modelling tools to create different surface textures. The fish tank is made by cutting out simple profiles from slabs of Plasticine and positioning them in a wooden frame. You must remember to work in reverse: what is on the righthand side when making will be on the left of the cast.

TROPICAL FISH

MATERIALS

Plasticine
Modelling clay
Latex
Plaster
Galvanized wire
Vegetable oil
Acrylic paint:
red, turquoise, blue
and white
Gold powder
Cellulose varnish

EQUIPMENT

Rolling pin
Baseboard
Modelling tools
Mixing bowl
Paintbrush
Old felt tip pen
Strips of timber
2in (5cm) oval nails
Small mixing dish

Roll out some modelling clay, making it thicker in the middle than at the edge. Lay a copy of the template provided on the clay and cut round it with a modelling tool.

Bevel the edge and smooth it with a wet finger. Use a wide-ended tool to slice off the top of each fin to lie lower than the main body.

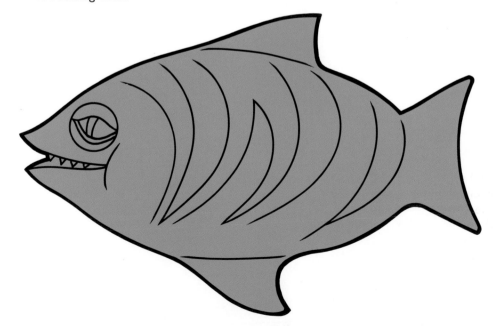

Flatten the area between the ridge marks drawn on the surface. Smooth these areas out with a wet finger so these three ridges stand proud.

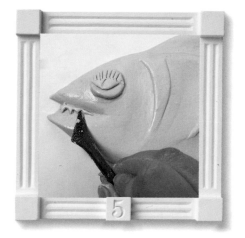

Shape the eye and create eyelash marks. Cut out a wedge for the mouth and bevel it. Make the teeth: notice how their shape has been determined by the shape of the modelling tool.

Using a serrated-edged modelling tool, on each of the raised ridges hold it at an angle and press lightly. With the sharp edge of a modelling tool make a series of cross-hatched lines on the fins and the tail.

Roll a small ball of clay and stick it in position for the eye, wetting the surface of the fish first. Blend the edges with a modelling tool to fix the join and smooth over with a wet finger.

84

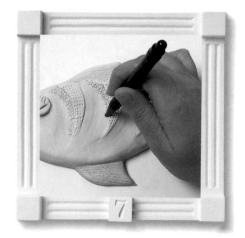

Press an old felt tip pen into the surface of the clay in between the ridges on the fish. You are now ready to make a latex mould (see page 14). Cast the fish relief into plaster.

To make a fish tank, make a wooden frame around the baseboard and seal the gaps between the frame and the board with Plasticine in the same way as for the mini-veg panel (see page 46).

Model a wavey shape of Plasticine 1in (2.5cm) thick and position it at the top of the frame. Cut out two $^{1}/_{2}$in (13mm) thick fish shapes and place these in the frame. Cut out thin wave shapes and place these around the fish.

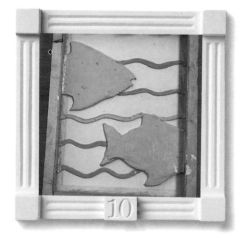

Coat everything with vegetable oil to prevent sticking and pour in the plaster slowly and evenly and incorporate hanging hooks.

Smooth the edges with sandpaper and then paint the whole tank blue. Paint darker blue into the recessed areas.

Paint the whole fish with scarlet red and allow to dry.

Brush deep violet red into all the crevices of the fish.

Mix some gold powder and cellulose varnish and paint the lips, teeth and eye lids. Paint patterns on the body in contrast with the indentation marks.

Add white to turquoise and paint the whole fish. Use turquoise straight from the tube to brush into the crevices. Apply gold powder and varnish as before but in different patterns.

**SHOELESS JOE • Shell box
and starfish box**
Plaster casts were taken
from an original shell and
starfish and glued onto
wooden boxes. The
painted surface of the
boxes was broken up by
sanding to produce a
weather beaten look.

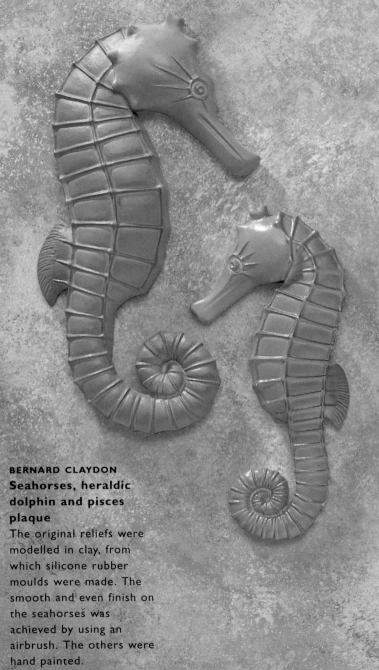

**BERNARD CLAYDON
Seahorses, heraldic
dolphin and pisces
plaque**
The original reliefs were
modelled in clay, from
which silicone rubber
moulds were made. The
smooth and even finish on
the seahorses was
achieved by using an
airbrush. The others were
hand painted.

► **THE WORKS • Shell clock**
Shells were bonded to a dome-shaped base to make the original. The verdigris finish was achieved by painting the cast dark red/brown and then sponging on turquoise randomly. Finally, it was brushed with gilt cream diluted with turpentine.

The variety of forms that exist below the sea are brought to life in this section. The wooden boxes

GALLERY

and mirror have a driftwood quality, a fitting match for their shell and starfish attachments. Sea creatures are very easy to model and cast, either as individual elements or as wall plaques, and together with shells make attractive border decorations. The anchor is a splendidly rendered traditional seafaring symbol.

SHOELESS JOE
Starfish mirror
The rough sawn timber frame was white-washed to reflect sun bleached beaches. Plaster casts were made from real starfishes and bonded to the frame. The natural sisal hanging rope further develops the seashore theme.

BERNARD CLAYDON
Humpback whale
The original whale was modelled in clay, from which a silicone rubber mould was made. The smooth and even finish was achieved by applying the colour with an airbrush.

THE WORKS
Shell mirrors
Shells were bonded to papier mâché frames, the smaller frame having a rope surround attached. The plaster casts were painted with burgundy coloured paint with gilt cream brushed on top.

JOHN DEVEUVE • Anchor
Modelled in clay, a rubber silicone mould was then taken. The mottled paint effect was achieved by applying the paint with an airbrush.

HEAVENLY BODIES

Stars, moons and suns are ideal shapes to make and cast, and can be used in a variety of ways. The Star Brooches are extremely easy to make and are cast directly from pastry cutters. The Eclectic Mirror is made by applying the plaster freehand with a variety of objects then embedded in it. The Twilight Box is made in a similar way but, instead of plaster, decorating filler is used into which a star and moon shape are embedded before the filler sets. Sun, moon, star and cloud shapes are perfect subject matter for a mobile. Each is painted with a hazy colouring to give them a far away look. The Sun Wall Plaque is decorated in five different ways, clearly demonstrating the wide variety of effects which can be achieved.

These brooches will add an extra sparkle to everyday dress. Moulds for the shapes are formed using baking cutters and Plasticine to contain the plaster when it is poured. The casts need to be removed with great care to avoid breaking them. Superglue is used to attach the brooch fasteners to the back of the casts.

STAR BROOCHES

MATERIALS

Plaster
Plasticine
Vegetable oil
Superglue
Brooch fasteners
Acrylic paint: gold, blue and silver
Bronze spray paint
Gold wax

EQUIPMENT

Pastry cutters, large and small
Rolling pin
Mixing bowl
Sandpaper
Small mixing dish
Paintbrush
Cloth

Carefully peel away the Plasticine, keeping the cutters in position. Hold the cutters and gently push the plaster cast and the small cutter through the large one.

Coat the inside of each cutter with vegetable oil. On a bed of Plasticine place a small cutter inside a larger one. Pour plaster into this mould and gently agitate to expel any air bubbles.

Hold the plaster cast and gently push the small cutter up through the cast. Use sandpaper to smooth the edges and glue a brooch fastener to the back.

Cast two solid shapes from the larger pastry cutter using the same technique. Smooth the edges with sandpaper.

Apply superglue to one of the stars and place the other on top, lining up the points of the top star between the points of the lower star.

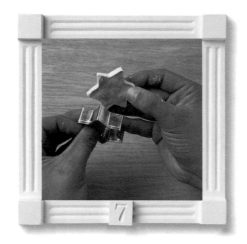

Make a solid cast of the small pastry cutter. Smooth the edges and then glue a brooch fastener to the back.

Hold the two stars firmly together until the glue has set and then glue a brooch fastener to the back.

Paint the first star cast gold and the smallest star silver. Paint the double star blue and allow to dry. Use a cloth to rub gold wax onto the surface.

Alternatively, use bronze spray paint to decorate the double star. Make sure that the spray reaches into the crevices between the two stars but also avoid making drip marks.

94 All the mobile elements were cast from purchased rigid moulds. Hanging hooks were embedded as part of the casting process. They are decorated using a sponge to produce a hazy effect – this gives the impression they are out of focus and a long way away. All the colours have been mixed with white to make pastel shades.

SKY MOBILE

Paint the cloud with a mixture of yellow and white paint. Allow all the elements to dry.

MATERIALS

Plastic moulds
Plaster
Acrylic paint:
white, blue, red,
yellow and gold
Dowelling wood
Chain or ribbon
Paperclips

EQUIPMENT

Small mixing dish
Paintbrush
Sponge
Toothbrush
Mixing bowl

Apply base coats to both sides of all the elements. Mix pink from red and white for the star; mix mauve from red, blue and white for the sun; and pastel blue from blue and white for the moon.

With a sponge dab white paint onto the surface, including the back. Allow to dry.

Dab pastel yellow paint onto both sides of each element. Allow to dry.

Load a toothbrush with gold paint and spatter the surface of each element.

Join two pieces of wood to form a cross. Attach each element to the cross with a length of chain or ribbon. Hang the whole mobile from the ceiling.

A night-time theme of moon and stars was chosen for this project. However, you could use other plaster casts – ready-made ones or those cast from moulds you have made or bought. Choose casts that will complement each other and produce a pleasing design. Do not select big and cumbersome casts as they will make the box difficult to handle.

TWILIGHT BOX

MATERIALS

Box with lid
Plaster casts of
moon and 2 stars
Decorating filler
Spray paint: black,
silver and red
Gold wax

EQUIPMENT

Filling knife
Mixing bowl
Cloth

Mix some decorating filler to the consistency of cream cheese and spread it over the lid.

Arrange the plaster casts on the lid of the box until you get a pleasing composition.

Apply filler to the back of the moon and two stars, position them on the lid and push down to obtain a good fixing.

Use a wet filling knife to smooth the filler around the edges of the casts, closing up any gaps.

Spray silver paint horizontally so the spray is not aimed at the surface but falls on top of it with the high points becoming coated with silver.

Alternatively, spray a red base coat and with a cloth dipped in gold wax wipe over the high areas of the lid.

When the filler has completely dried spray the lid, sides and bottom of the box with black paint. Allow to dry.

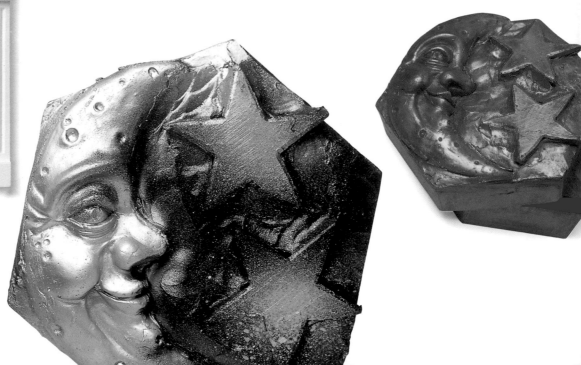

This mirror surround is made by applying plaster freehand. The plaster mix is left to thicken to the consistency of cream cheese before laying it. Plaster blanks and glass beads embedded in the plaster make a highly decorative and original mirror surround. It gives you the opportunity to creatively use some of those interesting objects you have collected over the years!

While the plaster is still wet carefully lay the mirror on top, applying light pressure to embed the mirror in the plaster. Allow the plaster to go off.

ECLECTIC MIRROR

MATERIALS

Plaster
Corrugated card
Newspaper
Mirror
Plaster casts: sun, moon and 3 stars
Glass beads
Black acrylic paint
Gold and silver powder
Cellulose varnish
Paperclip

EQUIPMENT

Mixing bowl
Palette
Paintbrush
Cloth

Cut corrugated card to the same size as the mirror and lay it on top of the newspaper. Mix some plaster. Hold the card in position and apply the plaster around, and just covering, the edge of the card to create a border 2in (5cm) wide.

Mix up a small amount of plaster and apply it along the top of the mirror. Lay a selection of your plaster casts and beads in the wet plaster and apply light pressure to ensure a good fixing. Run your finger along the inside edge of the plaster to make it even all around the mirror.

Continue creating the border around the mirror. Mix only a small amount of plaster at a time otherwise it will be wasted.

Paint the whole surface, back and front, with black paint. Mix silver powder with cellulose varnish and apply over the whole frame with a dry brush.

Mix together gold powder and cellulose varnish and paint onto parts of the beads and embedded objects in a variety of patterns.

Wipe away the excess plaster and leave to go off. When dry turn the mirror over and peel off the newspaper and card. Place a bent paperclip in a small amount of plaster at the top end to form a hanging hook.

This project encompasses Plasticine modelling, mould making, taking a cast and decorating. The cast can be decorated in a variety of ways: a bright yellow stippled finish emulates the shimmering sun in a blue sky and a solid bright yellow finish makes an even bolder statement; the cheerful ambience of the plaque is enhanced using silver or gold; and a sparkling sandstone finish gives a more natural effect.

SUN WALL PLAQUE

Roll two sausage shapes for the eyebrows, two balls for the cheeks and a smaller ball for the nose. Push them into the surface to form a face, blending them in with your fingers.

MATERIALS

Plasticine
Plaster
Latex
Acrylic paint:
yellow, cadmium
blue, Prussian blue,
white and silver
Textured acrylic
glitter gel
Red oxide paint
Gold wax

EQUIPMENT

Mixing bowl
Saucer
Modelling tool
Paintbrush
Small mixing dish
Sponge
Cloth

Knead the Plasticine and pat it out into a ½in (13mm) thick circle. Lay it on top of a saucer and add the rays of the sun, pushing them well into the rim.

Use a modelling tool to shape the facial details. You are now ready to make a latex mould (see page 14). Take a cast.

Paint the background areas between the sun's rays and the rim of the plaque a bright blue.

Paint the face yellow, reaching into all the crevices. Take care not to go over the edges onto the blue background.

Use a dry brush to emphasize the high points on the surface of the face with white paint.

Use a sponge to dab white paint on top of the blue.

Alternatively, mix a light blue from white and blue paint and with a sponge dab it onto the surface. Make sure that the paint reaches into all the crevices.

Mix white and yellow paint to make a lighter shade. With a sponge dab it lightly onto the surface of the face.

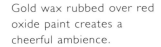

Enhance the high points of the face with darker blue paint by dragging a relatively dry brush across the surface.

Finally, stipple bright yellow paint over the entire surface.

Gold wax rubbed over red oxide paint creates a cheerful ambience.

Another alternative is to paint the background with deep Prussian blue.

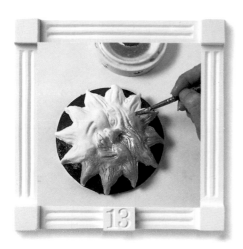

Paint the face with silver. Apply another coat of silver when dry to strengthen the effect.

To produce a sparkling sandstone effect, brush textured acrylic glitter gel over the whole surface of the plaque.

◄ **BERNARD CLAYDON**
Ivory moon and gold star
The original moon and star
were modelled in clay and
silicone rubber moulds made.
The smooth and even colours
were achieved by applying the
finish with an airbrush.

▼ **SARAH WILLIAMS**
Heart wall relief
Brightly coloured folk art
inspired the design of this
relief. It was handpainted
with acrylic paints.

▲▶ BERNARD CLAYDON
Verdigris stars
The original stars were modelled in clay. A combination of applying paint with an airbrush and handpainting was used to create a verdigris effect.

▲ THE WORKS • Sun clock
The precise and symmetrical design on this clock was painted on top of a white base coat using cobalt blue paint and gilt.

GALLERY

There is a limited selection of shapes available to us up in the sky but the vast variety of plaster objects that exist which use these forms is truly amazing. The sun and moon were the inspiration for a variety of wall plaques, mirrors and clocks. Stars have been blended with sun rays in other wall plaques and can be combined most effectively with hearts to form a border design for a mirror.

▲ THE WORKS
Squirls mirror
The original for this
mirror surround was a
wood frame with star
plaster blanks, string
spirals and hearts made
from Plasticine bonded to
the surface. A verdigris
finish was applied.

◀ ALAN WALLIS DESIGN
Sun mirror
The plaster cast was
painted light green over
which gold paint was
applied. This was then
rubbed back to reveal the
paint underneath it in a
patinated effect.

▶ **THE WORKS** • **Squirl heart**
The finish for this heart is verdigris:
dark red/brown paint was brushed
on and turquoise sponged randomly
on top. A coat of diluted gilt cream
was then applied.

▲▶ **BERNARD CLAYDON**
Yellow sun and gold sun
The originals for both of
these suns were modelled
in clay. The smooth and
even finishes were
achieved by applying the
colour with an airbrush;
they were then varnished.

In this chapter you learn the important technique of taking a one-piece (two-dimensional) mould from a three-dimensional object, in this case a Classical Statue. The intricately modelled Buddha Panel is cast from a ready-made mould. Two techniques are used to colour it, both of which produce an aged quality. The Cherubs are decorated in both metallic and bright, natural colours. A blank

FACES AND FIGURES

plaster cast of a Greek Bust is given a simplified marble finish as well as the almost surreal porphyry which clearly demonstrates the impact you can achieve from different decorative techniques. The Cherub Mirror is made using decorating filler into which plaster casts of cherubs are embedded. The black and gold finish produces an antiqued gold mirror surround.

110

A plaster cast of a Greek or Roman sculpture adds classical elegance to any room. Although usually decorated to complement their classical elegance, here it takes on a somewhat surreal air. The cast is first coated with matt spray sealer to prevent the paint from being absorbed by the plaster and then paint is spattered on. It is important to apply each colour evenly to the surface.

GREEK BUST

Use a toothbrush to spatter the cast with watery black paint and then again with white paint.

MATERIALS

Plaster bust
Acrylic paint:
purple, black, red,
white and gold
White spray paint
Silver marble spray
paint
Matt spray sealer

EQUIPMENT

Paintbrush
Sponge
Toothbrush

Cover the head thoroughly with matt spray sealer. Brush on purple acrylic paint using loose cross-hatched strokes. While the paint is still wet dab the paint surface with a sponge.

Mix white and red paint to produce a deep pink colour and spatter onto the surface as before. Repeat the technique using gold paint. Leave to dry.

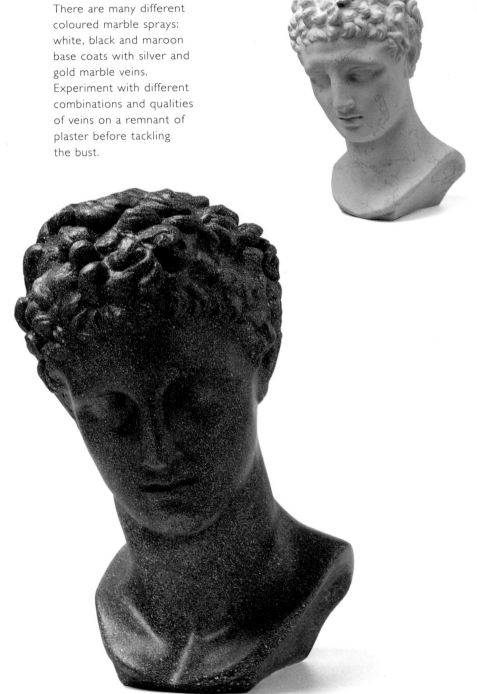

Apply matt spray sealer to seal the surface.

There are many different coloured marble sprays: white, black and maroon base coats with silver and gold marble veins. Experiment with different combinations and qualities of veins on a remnant of plaster before tackling the bust.

Special marble sprays are now available. Spray a white basecoat evenly over the whole bust. Use silver marble spray to add veins and blend these in more realistically by spraying a small amount of white on top.

112 Cherubs are widely available as casts and moulds. The winged cherub was sprayed black and gold enamel paint applied to the highlights with a cloth. Spray paint allows an even base coat to be achieved. The base colour of the other cherubs is a watery mix of acrylic paint, with highlights of gold and bright colours.

CHERUBS

MATERIALS

Plastic moulds
Plaster cherub
Plaster
Black spray paint
Gold enamel paint
Acrylic paint: red,
white, yellow, blue,
green and black
Gold powder
Cellulose varnish

EQUIPMENT

Cloth
Paintbrush
Small mixing dish
Mixing bowl

In a well-ventilated area spray the cherub black. Spray evenly backwards and forwards to avoid creating runs and drip marks.

Dip a cloth in gold enamel paint and run it over the surface of the cherub so the high points are coated with gold.

Mix white and red to make a flesh colour. Mix a darker tone and paint the crevices. Paint the wings turquoise, the hair yellow and the trumpet black.

You can have a lot of fun painting cherubs in a less traditional manner!

Mix gold powder with cellulose varnish and paint the trumpet. Brush gold lightly over the hair, wings and high points of the body with a dry brush.

114

This intricately modelled Buddha panel is the very essence of Indian art. It is an object for contemplation, not only of the subject matter but also the detailed modelling in each of the panels – each tells a story. A plaster cast is taken from a purchased plastic mould and then decorated. The antiqued metal finish enhances the relief forms and also gives the panel a museum-like quality.

BUDDHA PANEL

Mix burnt umber and Payne's grey paint and cover the whole of the panel. Leave to dry.

MATERIALS

Plastic mould
Plaster
Acrylic paint: burnt umber and Payne's grey
Bronze yellow paint
Irridescent bronze paint
Gold paint
Antique silver powder
Cellulose varnish

EQUIPMENT

Mixing bowl
Paintbrush
Sponge
Small mixing dish

Pour the plaster into the mould slowly and evenly. When it has gone off turn the mould and cast over and gently lift the mould off the plaster cast.

Mix bronze yellow and irridescent bronze paint. Dip a sponge in the paint and wipe it across the relief so that it picks out the high points.

Dip a sponge into gold paint and rub this over the central panel, with the high points again picking up the paint.

For an alternative finish, paint a mixture of antique silver powder and cellulose varnish onto the outer panels.

116

A three-dimensional ornament is transformed into an attractive wall plaque using a one-piece mould. A ledge of Plasticine is built around the object and undercuts are filled in to enable easy removal. The finish is verdigris, a term used to describe the surface of copper, bronze or brass objects which have been exposed to the elements. This colouring was chosen to complement the classical form.

CLASSICAL STATUE

MATERIALS

Statuette
Plasticine
Corrugated card
Latex
Plaster
Bronze enamel paint
Acrylic paint: blue, green and yellow
White emulsion
Whiting powder
Methylated spirits

EQUIPMENT

Mixing bowl
Paintbrush
Toothbrush
Cloth

Fill the space between the card and the underside of the statuette with Plasticine and build halfway up the statuette. You are now ready to make the latex mould (see page 14).

Knead the Plasticine to make it more pliable. Cut a piece of corrugated card to the height and width of the statuette and place it underneath.

Take a cast and brush on a coat of bronze enamel paint. When it is dry apply a watery mix of blue and green acrylic paint over the whole surface.

Mix white emulsion, light blue and bright green acrylic, whiting powder and methylated spirits to form a paste. Brush all over the surface and leave to dry.

Lightly brush the surface with water and sprinkle whiting over. Wipe off the excess.

Use a cloth to dab on some light blue acrylic paint and leave to dry. Make a watery mix of lime green acrylic and spatter it over the surface with a toothbrush.

118

The diamond hanging format of this classical style mirror adds a sense of drama and the gold finish makes it look antique. The frame and base are foamboard, available from art material suppliers, but if you wish to use a mirror larger than 15in (38cm) use a wood frame. The cherubs are bonded to the frame using decorating filler, which takes longer to set and sets harder than plaster.

CHERUB MIRROR

MATERIALS

Plaster cherubs
Foamboard
Mirror
Galvanized wire
Double-sided
adhesive tape
Decorating filler
Black spray paint
Gold enamel paint
Decorative paper
Brown parcel tape
Aerosol spray glue

EQUIPMENT

Cutting mat
Scalpel
Fine felt tip pen
Straight edge/ruler
Pliers
Mixing bowl
Filler knife
Cloth

Place this frame on top of the other piece of foamboard and line up the edges. Holding a pen at an angle, trace the inside square and then cut it out.

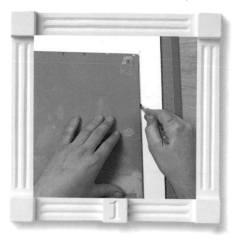

Cut two pieces of foamboard 2in (5cm) larger than the mirror. Place the mirror centrally on top of one piece and cut the board around the mirror.

On the larger frame make two slits 4in (10cm) from the same corner. Cut two lengths of wire and bend double. Push each loop through a slit so it projects 1in (2.5cm) on the other side. Bend the ends to lie flat.

Place double-sided tape along the edges of the smaller frame. Position the larger frame on top with the edges lined up and press to ensure the tape sticks.

Turn the frame over with the hanging hooks behind at the top. Arrange the cherubs on the frame in a pleasing design. Remove the casts, keeping them in the same composition.

Apply some filler to the underside of a cherub, position it on the frame and push to obtain a good fixing.

Rest the mirror on the flange you have created to make sure it fits. Trim the foamboard if necessary.

Support the frame above the work surface. Mix some decorating filler to the consistency of cream cheese and spread a layer over the frame.

Add more filler if necessary under the wings and wherever else the cherub does not come into contact with the filler.

Where a cherub hangs over the edge of the frame, apply filler underneath and level off to the frame edge to strengthen.

Turn the frame over and secure the two hanging hooks by applying them with filler. Use a knife to trim off excess filler along the flange of the frame. Leave to dry thoroughly.

In a well-ventilated area spray the back and front of the frame with black spray paint. Make sure one side is dry before turning the frame over.

Insert the mirror and secure in place with brown parcel tape.

Spray the back of the mirror with adhesive and smooth decorative paper over. Cut to the right size.

Dip a cloth in gold paint and gently wipe across the surface of the cherubs so the paint is picked up by the high points and the crevices remain black.

GALLERY

CLIFTON LITTLE VENICE
Greek head
A coating of black paint
was rubbed off before it
had completely dried;
notice how the paint has
been trapped in the
crevices to produce the
stone effect.

▲ DOPPELGANGER • **Piggy**
back climbing figure
This piece was inspired by
an actor seen rescuing a
person in a film. The
plaster cast was lightly
stained and varnished.

► **MATTHEW LEE • Roccoco wall clock**
This clock was inspired by Spanish and
Italian church interiors. The original
surround was modelled in clay, from
which a mould was made. The plaster
cast was painted black and
then applied with gold.

Classical sculpture from around the globe provides perhaps the
greatest inspiration of all. The human form has been rendered
throughout history by artists: the calm figure of buddha; the
beauty of Greek and Renaissance sculpture; the dramatic masks of
Roman theatre; the perenniel figure of the cherub; and the
experimental figurative sculpture of the twentieth century.

▲ **MARK LA TROBE • Cherubs**
Gold ink was painted over these
cherubs. Before drying it was
rubbed off the body, leaving a
residue in the crevices.

MIKE WELLS
Cherub mirror
A base colour was sprayed
on and gold wax was
applied to achieve an
antiqued effect.

MIKE WELLS • Eye
Gold wax rubbed over a
base coat of black paint
produces an alternative
effect to that of classical
sculpture.

▼ MARK LA TROBE • Buddha
Car paint spray was used
to create this extremely
authentic metallic finish.

MARK LA TROBE • Nose and mouth
These plaster casts, taken from classical
sculpture, were coated with clear wax
and then buffed to produce a creamy
surface shine.

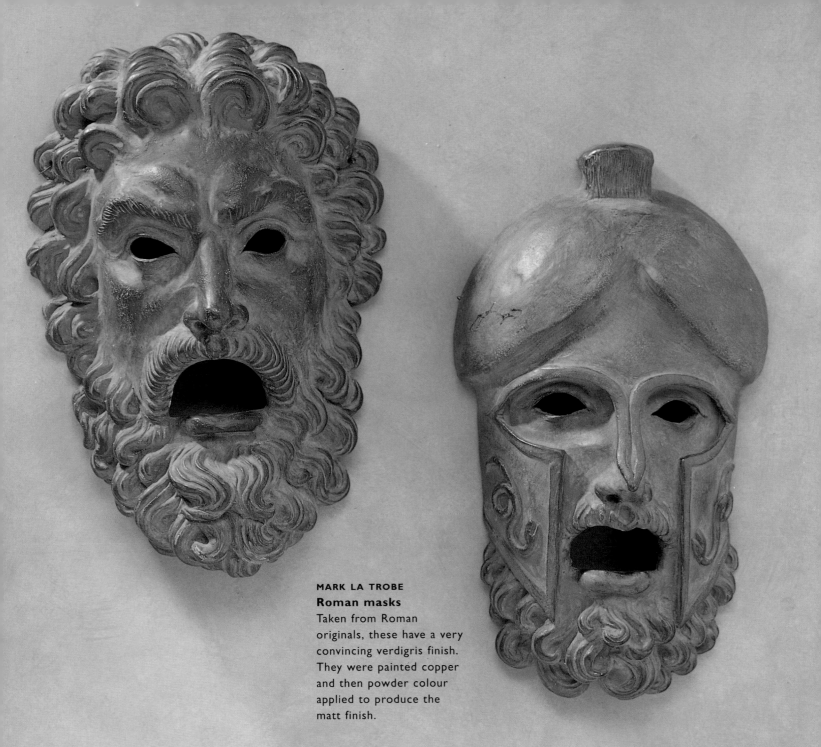

MARK LA TROBE
Roman masks
Taken from Roman
originals, these have a very
convincing verdigris finish.
They were painted copper
and then powder colour
applied to produce the
matt finish.

INDEX

CREDITS

Quarto would like to thank the following individuals who took part in the step-by-step demonstrations:

Ofer Acoo, Errol Allen, Clare Baggaley, Mary Fellows, Sandra Hurst Chico, Dhyan Jennings, Mark La Trobe, Karen Nettlefield, John Plowman, Mike Wells, Debbie Worth

Quarto would also like to thank all those who kindly submitted items for the gallery, including: Ofer Acoo, Clapton, London; Alan Wallis Design, courtesy of Ruth Gill Interiors, Crouch End, London; Kristina Bieganski at Funky Eclectica, Shepherd's Bush, London; Bernard Claydon, Brighton, Sussex; Clifton Little Venice, Maida Vale, London; John De Veuve at Rough Arts, Westcliffe-on-Sea, Essex; Rae and Lee Fether at The Works, Kentish Town, London; Mark La Trobe at Plasterworks, Islington, London; Matthew Lee at Larnaca Works, Grange Wale, London; Simon Sprecher at Doppelganger and Shaun and Nicole Keir-Tomalin at Shoeless Joe, both courtesy of Crocodile Antiques, Muswell Hill, London; Pamela Stewart-Pearson, Esher, Surrey; Julie Taylor and Maddy Petit at Mirabilis Design, Clapham, London; Mike Wells at Divine Decadence, Putney, London; Sarah Williams, Blackheath, London.

Finally, Quarto would like to thank the following suppliers who contributed materials for use in the demonstrations:

Alec Tiranti Limited
27 Warren Street,
London W1P 5DG, UK
Tel & Fax: 0171 636 8565

DecoArt
PO Box 386, Stanford KY 40484, USA
Tel: 606 365 3193
Fax: 606 365 9739

Formby's
825 Crossover Lane,
Memphis TN 38117, USA
Consumer help line: 1-800-F-O-R-M-B-Y-S

Fred Aldous Ltd
PO Box 135, 37 Lever Street,
Manchester M60 1UX, UK
Tel: 0161 236 2477
Fax: 0161 236 6075

Hobby Ceramicraft
Rotherwick, Basingstoke, Hampshire, UK
Tel & Fax: 01256 762461

Modern Options Inc
2325 Third Street,
San Francisco CA 94107, USA
Tel: 415 252 5580
Fax: 415 252 5599

Supercast Ltd
Hawthorn Avenue, Hull HU3 5JZ, UK
Tel: 01482 223398
Fax: 01482 228445

Swanson
1200 Park Avenue,
Murfreesboro TN 37129, USA
Tel: 615 896 4114
Fax: 615 898 1313
Orders: 1 800 251 1402